Therapeutic
Stitches
of a
Heartbeat

Ms Creoleness

DEDICATION

To those who have Lost themselves in
Love
Found themselves through Pain
and
Accepted themselves in Time.

ABOUT THE AUTHOR

ADRINA SMITH WAS BORN IN NEW ORLEANS, LA DECEMBER 1970 TO ALEX SMITH AND BETTY THOMAS. FOUND THE PASSION OF THE ARTS THROUGH HER GRANDFATHER, TERRY SOULE`, WHO ALLOWED LANGSTON HUGHES AND EDGAR ALLEN POE TO BECOME HER BEST FRIENDS AT THE AGE OF 9. EARLY EDUCATION WAS THROUGH CATHOLIC SCHOOLS UNTIL BEING A TEENAGER REQUIRED MORE INTERACTIONS WITH LIKE PEERS. ALWAYS FELT LIKE AN OUTCAST DUE TO THE KNOWLEDGE OF THE ARTS SO HER LOVE FOR WRITING CEASED FOR THE MOMENT. SHE HAS SERVED IN THE US ARMY, MOTHER OF 2, GRANDMOTHER OF 5 AND MEMBER OF SEVERAL NONPROFIT ORGANIZATIONS.

DUE TO GRAPHIC TIMES, THE SENSE TO LOSE SELF TO FIND SELF SEEMED TO BE THE BEST WAY TO UNDERSTAND SELF; WHICH ENSURED THAT THE TIME HAD ARRIVED TO ALLOW THE PEN TO ONCE AGAIN BECOME HER LOVER. THESE STEPS TAKEN THROUGH LIFE ENSURED THE TRAVELS WOULD NEVER GIVE HER FALSE HOPE OR EVEN INDULGE IN BEING A DREAM CATCHER.

"NO MATTER WHAT OTHERS THINK, SAY OR EVEN ASSUME ABOUT ME, I AM A SURVIVOR OF MANY THINGS BUT THROUGH POETRY I WILL FOREVER BE FREE OF BONDAGE"

FORGOTTEN CHILD

In the absence of loving self you allowed many things
to destroy
A once happy little girl that respected you into an
emotionless shell
The days of his presence never filled me with joy
But your eyes dared to see the neon light that glistened
"Mental/Emotional abuse lives here"
The cries in the night would awaken you like a mother
concern
As you viewed his shadow beside me
Not once questioned me but only his point of view of
the screams and tears
Self-taught independence to fight gravesite demons
Of pity, hatred and confusion of a stolen childish heart
I imagined the Medusa length hands touching without
the penetration
Until the Jordan River couldn't make me wholesome
again
Still, I was the liar, the confusion maker of your
pretended happiness
No matter how much love you gave the devil, he
sharpens his fork in the lives of others
Giving him a son provided no relief for my sleepless
nights
So I involved myself in imagination for a mirror of a
grin
Wishing for that day to crawl in my father's arms for
protection
But when and how can these lips pronounce the evil
and childhood lost
To the monsters that supposed to warn me from the
world
My father's life with me was worth more than the death
of him

Therapeutic Stitches of a Heartbeat

For my knees pray many "Our Fathers" to deaf saints in
my Cathedral
As I grew my skeletons buried in my soul to hate and
destroy
Not all men but only those with tentacles of disgraceful
sexuality exposed
Seasons change and thankful for the roses and thorns in
my view
Karma came many years later to give me consolation
Five shots as you reach for the Time Picayune near his
beloved banana tree
History of the so called community activist death
displayed neither tears nor suspects
I have decided to cloth the skeleton of 33 years
Not in any material of contempt but only understanding
the fabric of me
You see, the love that I never had only created a
stronger connection for mine
No man will ever invade the bond between daughter
and me
I believe in listening, observing and communicating
Always remember that that once forgotten child is now
an adult with an ignited TICK TICK BOMB!!!

CRACKED

I was introduced to you through an abundance of love
That your presence changed wicked crows into an
elegant dove
Which encouraged me to have faith and believe in the
man above
With both of you with me there's nothing I was afraid
of

Time grew and you fed me dosages of the Arts
From poetry to speech to music at the age of 9 was my
start
You have to be valuable mentally than physically I was
taught
Understanding, love and dissect yourself is the first part

I have seen every food and animal in the Boot that is
exotic
And how we would laugh because I will never be
aquatic
Become my own person, not with the flow or even
robotic
For my presence in the world would soon be a justified
narcotic

As an adult we seemed to lose all sense of time
Due to being a provider and rolling hills to climb
Trying to keep my Creole Heritage and culture alive
more than just part-time
For the blood delivered to my Prince and Princess, yeah
it's sublimed

I allowed the ways of the world to be separate from you
Just couldn't let you know, I let you down as I was
going through

The love and life of acceptance through someone else's
view
Those traits you taught need review but I had to grow
into

But that call came and said you were gone
How could they do this since 2 weeks had long drawn?
For the pain, they knew I wouldn't be able to carry on
Without your words and love, I am deeply withdrawn

It has been 12 years and it haunts me everyday
For the things we didn't do and words I didn't say
But my love was deep but will never want to display
To another of fear of them dying or just to plain walk
away
But I will never be an actress with a scene to portray
Without standards, respect and honesty, no room for the
gray
But the healing from the loss like watching the bloom
of assorted flowers in a bouquet
It takes a hell of a man to fill Terry Soule's shoes,
Master Creole Cook, my Grandfather
New Orleans made, Love at Grade A.

MY VOICE OF REASONING

How can I begin these thoughts?
To express my feelings and respect of the
transformation of the mind.
The heart knew from the very first encounter
That I would understand true love, that Agape Love of
what God had bestowed upon me.
The moment I felt you, I knew you were mine.
You weren't just my beginning but you would be my
forever.
The soul couldn't grasp that emotion or concept
Since it wasn't told, expressed or shared but only felt
distressed.
Life had another plan for me drenched in stones but it
was turned into flowers with your smile and touch
I taught you that chivalry is never dead no matter the
shock of pain.
You are my first rose started from a seed and you grew
internally
Until the lessons flowed externally and it was given
back to me.
My cycle ceased from rejuvenating when I held you in
my arms
Looked into your eyes and vowed
That the rape and separation that disembodied my soul
and mind would not eat me

Therapeutic Stitches of a Heartbeat

But you allowed my heart to beat, to beat, only to beat
to love you how I wanted, needed and deserved.
My respiration no longer a complication
Since the relation that brought consolation
Encouraged a foundation of true motherhood, education
and mature transformation.
No longer concerned with character assassination,
demoralization, depreciation or even discrimination
Now it is time for your obligation of a presentation and
communication
With your seeds to ensure my grandchildren
understands and applies logical implication, natural
elevation and self-determination.
These genes possessed are like a corporation with
aspiration, celebration and strong heredity obligation
There will never be a vaporization in the sensation of
inspiration and consideration in this conversation
Just merely stating the facts of what I contributed to the
next generation.

Always remember that the love between a MOTHER
and her SON needs no explanation.

Ms Creoleness

I LIVE HERE

She was so insecure and naive
Of the world and life around
Not realizing she deserved better
From the cycle surfaced and surround
Changes in womanhood brought tears
To close to the point of breaking down
Mentally scorned from sense of loneliness
Tired of the turbulent ups and around

Never wanted to speak up
For fears of being misunderstood
Lashes revealed inside and out
Holding on to the lies being told
But this time she slept and I came to see
The one behind the abuse and insanity
Awakened by the words of power
Hibernation disturbed in his sleepful hour

No need to be alarmed
Cause I have lost interest in your games
Hair has changed and demeanor is rough
No need to share my purpose or even my name
Ring has been trashed and new rules apply
One of us will comply to the terms
Nonsense is over and chapter is revised
The old girl is gone "YA Heard"

Respect is the word of foundation
Be brave Dear, see the tables have turned
Faith and fidelity will be the gear
Adrina has disappeared and now Ms Creoleness
lives here.

THUG LOVE

He stood 6"2 with caramel skin with the sexiest accent
Presence that claimed attention
Bodybuilding physique with teeth
That stood toe to toe like the sun.

Spoke with control and defiance
Capturing every woman in his path
Never understood why to this very day
He wanted to be with someone like me

He brought me adventure second my month
Until my heart shook with every word
Deserving him was an understatement
My level of my love just wasn't enough

The same reason I feel in love, I fell in hate
Abuse, lies, and control
Became more than hugs, kisses and happiness
I will never forget about the person
Who swore to never hurt me or my family
But sometimes you have to pay the price
For enjoying the life of Thug Love.

AM I REALLY LOVED?

He Loves Me
Well that is what he told me last night
As I snuggled under him within the moonlight
Realized before the alarm that he was gone

See, this relationship defines me
Because of his love
I mean I love him more than I loved myself
I breathe for him because of him

He loves me
Even though the concealer has been emptied
Not able to hide the love
He provides when I am right or wrong

My scars are no longer external
Diminished internally through my bone marrow
I am trapped
I am controlled
But I love him

He loves me
Through text messages and phone calls of my
whereabouts
His concern is genuine
I know there is no one to love me like this

As I lay in this mysterious location
Tubes, gauges and machines working tremendously
Where is he
Where is his love

Two weeks have passed
Appears is the knight to this damsel in distress
Who longs for acceptance, validation and assurance?
His presence is gone again before the alarm

I attend to him in all ways
But my insides screams differently
The calls have changed
The text messages are 2 word answers
I am lost
How did I come to this?
My heart chiseled slowly

Keys turned
Lies heard of a hectic day
Instead of a kiss a fist provided the hello
Not today
Not anymore
I love me
I love me enough to shed blood to protect my heart
I have accepted the pain
Now it is time to let the woman he spends most of his
nights
Become His Love.

WHY?

Why are you looking at me?
As if I am the damn stranger
I was there from the start
But your actions were harsh and my love is in danger

Never thought I would go through this
The very thing that is defined as bullshit
Giving my evenings of reasons but it was only treason
Loving me was impossible throughout the seasons

But you constantly denied about being with that Bitch...

Somehow someway you constantly drew me in
Like Family Guy and SpongeBob embedded in my skin
With what, for whom...Fuck it...Why?
You gave me a mental, physical and emotional black
eye.

Do I really make you happy?
Years of tears shed changed my hair straight to nappy

Is a little given not enough or too much?
Getting disgusted by your presence and your touch
Is this my destiny from Mother Earth?
Or a hurtful lesson for a long overdue rebirth?

I am worth more than a thrill
Or is my thrill all I am worth

How can you enjoy both minds by not confusing the
hearts?
Guess you never thought I would finally get smart
To me being seen, known or treated as your spare part.

Therapeutic Stitches of a Heartbeat

Sometimes feeling like a bird on the wire
Waiting for someone to notice me, yeah the fire
Constantly engulfed with an addiction from my supplier
Need a cease fire
So I can be inspired, rehired and admired
Than just a sexual desire

Dying from the pride inside
Of a dream collide
Since my worldwide
Turned upside down from a love from this
motherfucker Mr. Jekyll and Dr Hyde.

Like a fool just entertaining your family and friends in
my face
All the while being played and disgraced
You were supposed to be my husband, you know my
soul mate
But I was just additional meat to cover your plate.

Am I confused?
Delirious or amused
Of being abused, confused and misused?
No, the hell I am not
You see the turbulence of keeping my sanity
By disrespecting my womanity
Instead I will use a little more profanity

These childish ass motherfucking mind games are
driving me crazy
Making my peripheral hazy
To make you smell nothing but black fucking daisies

But I sincerely thank you, because I can walk away
No more technical fouls on this running play
I am so much brighter from your charcoal grey
Of the pain inflicted as a tenant, yeah you were an
overstay
Enjoy your life now asshole, sooner or later Karma will
visit you day by day by day.

AGAIN

As I sit and endure the pain
Of the steps and bumps of loving again
I see where I went wrong
By giving all of so strong

Of course, I lost the sense of life
Trying to please you and to do what's right
Permission to arrange me into disarray
Feeling like a poodle being led astray

Thought I was hurtful and ashamed without you
Because of the epitome of loneliness that grew
Not knowing the preparation of epiphany
No concept of R&B, Jazz and Blues

Instead I found her and lost you
I simple price for peace of mind
Accepting the joys and pain of me, myself and who's
Heart no longer had me on a grind

She speaks in a whisper at night
To ensure transformation from gloom to light
Life is brighter more than before
Knowing another opportunity was at the door

This time I opened without self-doubt
Not concerned with the past to be ashamed to haunt
Finally saw the person I forget
How wonderful it is to love me Again!!!

GOOD MORNING

Good morning heartache
You have once again awakened me
From the smile that once was planted in my soul
But instead this emptiness is a mirror to what's in the
heart.

Good Morning heartache
My mind is in an uproar
Of the turbulent affairs that was shared just to be called
"ONE"
But you had to change the rules and now loneliness is
shared.

Good Morning Heartache
I am tired of your constant ache and pains
That you need to prove that you exist
This feeling has been for years but it's fresh like a fruit.

GOOD MORNING HEARTACHE
Thank you for this emotion
It proves I am not dead inside
And I can still feel..

FOR HIS LIFE

Blessed with ancestors who loved our heritage
But abandoned dreams for nourishing future souls
They had to fight to receive a better life
When segregation and racism was in flight
Our forefathers fought an enormous fight
For some to try to demolish our mission and blind our
sight.

What is the anger behind "Brown?"
When some can't tell the up from down
Of us to be around, they're astounded.
By the mental capability of our mind
That reminds of our struggles to move forward with
mankind.

Is it the food we eat?
Or the stride of our feet?
Thought we were protected of variety to meet
Socially concentrating to overcome defeat
I understand the word "destiny"
Refuse to stay in my home with no privacy
So we need to regroup and redefine our legacy
For the explosion of better me, you and we.

Too many crimes that try to paralyze and analyze
The presence of being demoralized
And our views are chastised, despised and criminalized
To be different but the same blood flows
Hungrily for admission of acceptance
Without judging a person by the appearance

Ms Creoleness

Fortunate to be created but the grain that precedes us
History, culture and language used as weapons of
unjust
To allow the body to be succumbed
But the worse disease "Hate" to us
Values should be hereditary not disgust

My grandchildren are my breath
And I am trained for my chest
To rise and fall to protect
So I refuse to let anyone or anything of any color to
contaminate and infect.

MY TWIN

It has never been a secret that I didn't want to have
children
Afraid of being a failure as a Parent
Blessed with a bundle of joy 2 years earlier
Couldn't let him grow up without a sibling

I prayed for someone else to love me
Walk like me
Act like me
Look at me

HE heard me and allowed my words to come into
existence
Even though morning sickness for 6 months was rough
Three trips to False Laborville
But we waited patiently for her arrival

Beautiful baby girl with a smile that can dry up the
Atlantic Ocean
Welcoming eyes that was warmer with each blink

Yes, she looks exactly like
Me

She grew up as the shadow of her brother
Not because she had to be with him
But she thought when I wasn't around
She needed to protect him

Yeah, she acts like
Me

Ms Creoleness

Excited with dismantling computers and various music
Not the typical child but she felt like an outcast in
school and home
Even though love poured through the walls
She struggled with her own presence

Yeah, she felt like
Me

Through years of tears
Mother/daughter talks
And that hurtful path of life was endured with each
other
Topics that may not have been shared until comfort
level was ensured

Heart of pure gold
Attitude like the weather
Stubborn worse than a mule
My Twin

We struggled through exasperating moments
Until no one knew our pain
But soaked pillows, used tissue
And
Us

She gave me glue to a broken piece
Of the back bone that was shattered
We have permanent jokes that no one could imagine
Only we understand the pitch line of our sense of
humor

Now she has given birth to her own bundle of joy
That makes me smile as the roles are now reversed
Increased the generation of role models being in the
home
I am so proud of her and the nurturing being passed on

She had grown from this misunderstood dorky kid
To a tremendous Mother and Daughter
Our relationship strives through honesty, turmoil,
arguments and sickness
She evens hear my voice in her head before she speaks

Taught and proven
To
"Believe in yourself no matter how many times you
stumble"
"No matter what you accomplish, stay humble"
"Don't allow anger to break your dreams"
"Be determined"
"Sometimes you have to say FUCK EM"
 And above else
"I am always beside and behind you."

My Goofy Twin

Love,
Mom

Ms Creoleness

COURAGE

Who has the courage to love again?
When pain and hurt is all within
Who has the words for a broken heart?
To prevent the bloody tears pouring from the start

No matter how hard I want, I cant
Because of lies, abuse and sin
Was it normal or just to be?
Without a mind to think or words to speak

Years of self-doubt about love for me
And of course the fear of being lonely
Cause hatred and numbness in my skin
To mean the words, hell to say them to blend

Nights are being fought in my dreams
Confused but strong enough not to relive
The feeling and reality of feeling all alone
But moving forward with thoughts to grow on

For now I will keep myself together
Pride, beauty and stern about it
To be able to intertwine without seeing him
I will have the courage the love again

ON THIS DAY

My heart bleeds more than beat
and this is hard for me just to admit
But the attraction of how we seemed to connect
Stuns me knowing of our concerns to just commit

My feelings are sincere willing to put time in it
Our emotions need constant repair from life's tool kit
You are very important intelligent with questions to
transmit
Before engaging in the physical, we should have
applied for love's work permit

Sometimes I can pout or even throw a fit
But I am brand new with you and you encourage me
never to quit
My mind and heart in a serious double knit
The more I pull away from you, the more entangled I
get

When we make love, you always put your leg in it
The only comparison is the white powder just
sniffing it
You should just let it go with no sentence. Just acquit
But my name is in chorus, no matter how you say it

Ms Creoleness

From our first encounter I was willing to submit
To the wants, desires and needs of this sinking tar pit
The handwriting on my skin is the epitome of legit
But the distance has changed roses to thorns and
happiness to shit

No need to play or convince through a lie
But my soul needs more through my teary eye
You will always share my love, no price to buy
But as of today, "I have to say GoodBye".

P T S D

I am Patiently Trying to Save my Destiny because
I AM NOT A HOPELESS VICTIM!!

So don't patronage me with an explanation
Trying to validate your lies is not my intention
Or to be a Veteran who is a statistic or an emotional
hostage
By entertaining ignorance of my justification
Of how I was chosen with this disease, condition or
sickness
With medication or professional concern

Life will go on whether it is disguised
From hurt of isolation, avoidance and paranoia or you
But my life is not to be materialized
So for nonsense I am just not available
Stay away from me
With your one dimensional pity
Of hat emotion I can't display
See because of the uniform, life and love
I was formed to be this way.

I AM NOT A HOPELESS VICTIM

You are still masquerading in a judgeful world
I am not afraid to be misunderstood from
My Rage, love, RAge, joy, RAGe, lust or RAGE
But I am still intelligent but it is shadowed
With a mental and psychological struggle
My face may express all of my feeling internally
Severely dying and trying to fight this demon
constantly

The demise of closing my eyes is still in question
Battling with good and evil to survive daily
Which causes me to connect, with my own defect
That sometimes I see me as it pertains to me
Mirrored as a product of the living dead

I AM NOT A HOPELESS VICTIM

I can accept the fact because I am tired of this act of the
life and its stage
Waiting for an applause of my fallen accomplishments
or footsteps
Since I no longer need a façade of my worth, hurt or
admission
I can chose you to know me, manifest with me
Grow with me, understand me and to love me in spite
of me
I refuse to be an accessory of your mindly prostitution
Of giving me unexpectedly but only you
Concern with disinterest of this unknown solution
No longer willing to love in a social purgatory
One day, you should sit and have a glimpse of my
healing story
Where do you stand in the mental struggle?
With spiritual wickedness traveled in the jungle
For some to only want to walk with a vocal muzzle
Afraid to be expressive to family and friends that can
leave them puzzled
Learning to have a piece of a peace of mind
With the identity of PTSD but I just want to save my
own destiny
Anything is possible, grab able and attainable you see
On the right path to a better me, a freer me

SO, I AM NOT A HOPELESS VICTIM

A mother of two and grandmother of five
Friend to few and enemy to many, I am loved
Loved from my obstacles achieved
Strong willed maintain but tears flow more than blood
Again, I am not a hopeless victim
But a survivor with acceptance of the world
Perception resting, eating inside of this once little girl
My war isn't with you but self
So, am I a hopeless victim?
Hell, no but held captive in a boat of indecision
Of the situation of confusion of darkness from your
mental circumcision
Where is your tip?
I am a realist but you hide behind others because you
fear me

SO, WHO IS REALLY THE HOPELESS VICTIM?

I am sometimes regressed and rebelled but isn't my
decision to display
Just sometimes find it hard to say, "I am okay"
Take some time to drink from the stream in my mind
To evaporate my sickness with your expressive essence
It just may really have you afraid of the possession of
my presence.

Hopeless Victim, Hell no, I am just a SURVIVING
VICTIM OF YOU!!

Ms Creoleness

GOOD BRIDGE EVIL

Today, I awakened in a pool of blood
Searching for my head and right leg
Not sure of the events transpire from yesterday
Alarm clock sounded
Sweat drenched sheets
Another nightmare.

Today, I haven't slept
I am not tired or delirious
Just mentally incapacitated from life
I just don't want to live

I am standing in my room
Walls seems to screech
Names of failure
I know you can't tell
I am at the end of trying any longer

Tears shed like a cocoon
Not to form a butterfly
But a decayed caterpillar

I just don't want to live anymore!!!!

Should I grab my keys?
Jump in the bed with my favorite girls?
Or
Stand still?

My presence is now in the kitchen
Not of hunger
But knives and scissors
Play by play action
Timing
Severity
I wouldn't want them to find me like this....

Back into what seems to be my demise
My thoughts filled the sounds of the television
Scanning over furniture
Boxes
Hair
Weight
Bank account
Car
Eyes
All of me
The disgust fills my stomach
No longer imaging anything good about myself
I am the bile within my body

I am nothing!!!!

Eyes swollen
Due to the independence
Financial security
Smile
Destroyed from turning the other cheek
Stab wounds to the chest/back
And
That misused word
Love

Ms Creoleness

Reflection in the mirror began to speak to me
"You are not worth a damn"
"You have demolished the triangle"
"You should ease the pain of others and die"
"You will never rebuild nor succeed"
"No one wants to hear your voice"
"You will never be anyone's rib or backbone"
"You are just worthless"

Shadow on the wall quickly interjected,
"This is only another trial to overcome"
"Be strong"
"Don't allow them to drag you down"
"Breath"
"Think clearly"
"Breath"
"Adrina, Adrina (screaming) ADRINA"?

By this time
Keys are in hand
I leave quietly
No wallet
No phone
Just Me
Tears
Interstate
25, 35
55, 70
90

I don't want to live anymore!!!!

Therapeutic Stitches of a Heartbeat

Swerving in & out of traffic
Either crash into the guardrail
Or
Plummet into the water
All of a sudden
Car stops
This must be my exit

I stand on the guardrail on the HRBT..

Voice on the left whispers
"Adrina, baby, come down"
"Wipe your tears to see clearly"
"Don't do this to your children/grandchildren"
"You have more reasons to live then die"
"Think about the people you have touched"

Voice on the right screams
"Everything you touch is ruined"
"Jump, Adrina, Don't be a fool, just Jump"
"Children/Grandchildren will be better off without you"
"What the fuck, Bitch jump, you are a weak ass
woman"
"JUMP"

Out of the waters
My granddaughter appears with open arms
Smiling
Saying
"Nawni, where are you"
"Nawni, hold me"

Jumps back in car
Sirens, honks seemed erratic
I ceased normal movements for 15 minutes

90, 70
55, 35
25
Gently opened the door
Hugged my favorite girls in their bed
Tears drying
Finally
Fell asleep
Tomorrow is another day
For
Self-Love
Healing
And
Rebuilding

BUTTERFLIES

Singing (One Man can make all women hate all men)

Yeah that used to be my theme song
Safer to have hatred and contempt because I was afraid
to move along
Because of this selfish ass motherfucker wanting to do
wrong
I admit, I allowed that Bullshit.
Woosah Woosah, but thanks to Anger Management
classes I am strong

No need to be rescued from my own bomb blast
You see, I know myself worth and it's not valued as a
jackass
My heart and soul has broken through and emotional
cast
But I am a survivor, a Soldier, and this too shall pass

I know there are many not a few of good men
Well, that's what I tell myself time and time again
We all travel with baggage and to be honest and only
then
Will you be able to unpack to the worthy but who has
the deciding pen

Ms Creoleness

To keep track of all of the ones who caused me unjust
While my veins no longer pump blood but instead drips
rust
Simply one-sided, cold-hearted and didn't want to
discuss
How someone can help me though the pain shit it's like
perfecting tips of a pie crust

This man will admire me more than most
He is serious about being my King and not just shining
the Queen's post
So appreciative of the battle wounds from love once
was diagnosed
He will keep me smiling like a kid with PB&J on toast

I am the only operator that holds the command and key
Of course I know that with love and life nothing is
trouble free
But when it happens you will be happier than watching
NFL Network on Direct TV
Or maybe like an incredible itch calmed from a dog flea
Swept away from the wind and almost drowned by the
sea

Therapeutic Stitches of a Heartbeat

Pretty soon I will find someone, yeah, my permanent
Golden Shower Tree
More like my exotic cream to fulfill this Creole Coffee
Taken daily for enrichment like a dose of Vitamin C
For those who are still angry and can't let go of destiny
The path will always have obstacles and swarming with
bees
Don't be upset for those having the guts to flee
Better yet, I won't let the past dictate me presently
This Butterfly's scars are now history.

FINALLY

When the winds refuse to give me a breeze
That could possibly eliminate the fire from spreading
I need water to consume the internal flame
Allowing my desire to succumb me is like watching the
clouds darkening.

Before the local news reporting of that drastic tornado
This will allow all demons to ride the wings of angel
thoughts
What is worse? To fight with others or with self
The woods can never express the feelings of my total
turmoil
Until the words bubble with anticipation of watching
my own decay

Mirror has no reflection of what I should see or be
Reminiscing of the smile that took over my soul
Only thing displayed is a grin of uncertainty
Have you ever felt lost?
Lost with no map, compass or GPS
To allow the reroute of the wrong path traveled
No one to be a backseat driver to alarm you before a
crash
You see, we all need a rewind or redo button
But will we have the audacity to know when to let go

Pain is in the depth of eyes, spoken and revealed
But the sweetest of dreams instantly changed to the
maggots of reality
So from time to time, my tears have a taste of vodka
From the selective ones of distilled betrayal

Therapeutic Stitches of a Heartbeat

My aura used to attract like a whiff of Euphoria
Only thing revealed is an empty bag of Purina
Never thought my shoes would no longer be filled
With the socks, pantyhose and feet of a troubled soul

My steps are moving in circles but my shadow is at a
standstill
Only movement is the manuscript provided to you
This pen caresses the pad like the dew on a sunflower
No matter of the world around, I smile with my heart

The ice has melted from my mind and soul
So as I plan this last note to my loved ones
I know my presence may have been misunderstood by
some
But I can now close my eyes and know
I am finally feeling the love

Ms Creoleness

FORGIVE ME

I am sorry for staying around so long
Thinking that things would change
For allowing my time to be used
By the unfortunate ones that just never understood

I am sorry for covering the bruises of mishaps
But constantly falling victim to hand held excuses
For accepting the words from guilt
Even though the actions were no fault of mine

I am sorry for the long talks between hearts
And mind that never once included the real you, your
soul
For letting Father Time instruct
Your tears to overflow through unnecessary pain

I am sorry for the glare of the sun and moonlight
To see you more than I saw myself
For diminishing my faith in believing
And also escaping for achieving

I am sorry for using all of your positive Youthful
energy
For just a latitude of negative memory
Watching years of onset maturity
To create a woman with high gullibility and insecurity

I am sorry for keeping your presence in a dusty and
concealed box
But WOW, I can see how you have grown through
those mental and psychological Locs

Therapeutic Stitches of a Heartbeat

I have accepted my own apology
By first allowing me to just be Me

Now I can possibly display all of desires and wearing it
firmly on my face
No concerned pleasing anyone but me at any time,
person or place

I have finally learned to begin the process to just
forgive myself.

TEARS

My tears flow en I am at a peak
Those others may never want to reach
A peak where others pain are seen
Through the eyes of the unknown
Emotion as diminished due to series of trails and
obstacles

My tears flow like the dew in the morning
Sprinkled across the unrecognized creation
Never reviewed for a second thought
Only for the dampness on a human finger
Still unsure of the perception of life within reality

My tears flow like the worse of an avalanche
Bothered by the unforeseen circumstances
That covers the mountains of a face
Displaying by damage and death internally
With turbulent periods of abandonment and neglect

My tears flow from the Rings of Saturn
That allows the planets to stand in amazement
Due to the outer shape and decorative style
Of what others fear my gravitation to be seen
How the stars surround me like people watching
And waiting for a fallen event to rejoice

My tears flow from my soul
Of many years of maintaining a positive façade
That humility by the divinity eaten away
But trying to cleanse my ducts of dirt and pain
Eroding reality infected from delusional ideals
From the water upon the once secured umbrella
That keeps me dry from this inclement weather of life

Therapeutic Stitches of a Heartbeat

My tears flow from the depths of the oceans
Through high tide to reach a solution of a shore
A place where others admire the view
But could never admit to the currents felt within
To see me through the variety of wavelike expressions
Still confused on whom to allow witnessing them
I am only a singular board of my own vessel.

My tears flow from the valves of my heart
For the ones I have touched with the impact of love
Maintains the action of determination
Tears cleansing my impurities collected like the dust on
glass
Through constant wiping until the outer surface is
appealing

Tears for the times wasted on and shared by the known
enemy
Tears appreciated for the events experience with those
close to me
Tears shed for the ones with whom my genuine spirit
refuses to have pain
My tears flow constantly within me but when it needs
to break the dam it has no other way to be seen but in
my dreams

And I still somehow, someway wear a smile through
my and your abundance of tears.

Ms Creoleness

THE 1

I stand here to speak on behalf of her
The person that some have crossed beneath her flower
The one whose presence could offset the clouds
And words that mingles with laughter and confusion

I stand here to speak on behalf of her
Though my tears stumble upon each other
My voice may be muffled
But on this day you will finally know and appreciate
her

She is the one who tried out for the basketball team
Not knowing how to even dribble or even block
She is the one who decided that debate would be best
Because at home, words and feelings were lost

She is the one always felt misunderstood and an outcast
For being knee high to a caterpillar and sky high to a
toddler
But always had her head in a book but naive to the
common
She didn't know the other senses came with such a high
cost

She is the one, raped and mother claimed that she was a
whore
But she never missed a day of school while water and
birth flowed on graduation day
She is the one who walked the halls in college with the
above
For he was the one who showed her how to see and feel
love

Therapeutic Stitches of a Heartbeat

She is the one who married not to ever to be a single
parent
But the bond created through motherhood still left her
singular
She is the one who raised her right hand for country and
children
But deployments, field exercised would keep them
apart

She is the one who decided that years of servicing that
the children needed to come first
Took off the uniform finally and attending PTA
Meetings, Violin Recitals, Plays, ROTC Competitions
and Track
Is what kept the glowing upon her face

She is the one described as loving, funny, alpha female
and down to earth by some
And cold, nonchalant and moody to others
She is the one who believes in truth without the
reactions or actions of others
But still has no idea to find the words for her own
emotions

She is the one who worked exceptionally hard at her
career and love
But lost herself trying to please them both
She is the one who still would fight the wind for true
friends, yeah her SHIPmates
Even though, few in numbers, some to have never met
but thinks of them daily

Ms Creoleness

She is the one who smiles for and with you
But no one knows her constant tears within
So I stand here not because of her expiration
But hopefully soon enough, you would have finally
appreciated the journey between the blood and her ink

This is my own Memorial....

GREEN-EYED MONSTER

A closed mouth don't get fed
But an opened one consumes too much
They always say that the eyes are the pathway to the
soul
How can it be if it is shadowed by the Green Eyed
Monster?

This person affects the wealthy and the poor
College graduates and high school diplomas
Military and civilian and all shades of skin and religion

Jealousy, insecurity and low self-esteem allows this
monsters eyes
To sparkle in the night and darkened during the day
These are the people we love the most
Share our deepest secrets
Lay beside us during slumber
But do we really know if our best interests are kept in
their grasp?

In the quest to be accepted for the battle wounds of life
Instead enables them to throw the very stones
That we wished to stay buried
The ones we love the most sometimes hurt us the worst

Never allow someone's words to deter your smile
Never allow someone's success to burn the path to your
journey
Never allow someone's struggles to bury your purpose
Never give up on yourself, no matter the times of
stumbling
Never compromise yourself for the happiness of others

Ms Creoleness

I, as a woman will always bloom
No matter how many times the monster throws dirt on
me
For every garden has assorted flowers to admire
But can be easily be unappreciated and slandered from
the weeds and thorns surrounding them

So let the Green Eyed Monster continue his or her
mission
For this rock refuses to stoop to childish tactics.

Continue to talk on Monster, for your words are the
encouragement not to be like you.

LOC'D UP

Amazed of the Queen's natural crown
Enhanced mental and spiritual growth
That entailed more than strength and self-determination
Dismantling of worldly views.
Standing as an individual
Not posed on Ebony or Vogue
In hope of a runway model contract
Or cosmetic debut with Covergirl or Victoria Secret
I am released from the confinement of that bullshit ass
box.

My inches show my history
Of forgotten trails within my closet
The remembrance of the struggles
From childhood to adulthood is free among the length
Being lockup encouraged
The process of loc'd up
Unveiling who I truly am from a simple strand of hair
I am a feminine Samson with the power within my head
Allowing my spirits to flourish among my follicles

Not concerned about life's rendition
Outside clarification
Or movements to be validated
I have been set free from an internal storm
Replenished from the eye of the hurricane and its
destruction

I am PASSIONATELY
PERSISTENCE
IN THE PERSEVERANCE
OF MY

LOCS!!!!

POET vs PERSON

I often sit in a dark room
Trying to face myself
Wanting to be alone for awhile
Separate from crowds, family, new people
Family, strangers
Cries more than the sun shines
Not because of unhappiness
But fear
Of what I have become

I sit with constant thoughts
Writing more than my mind can articulate
Scheduling for events and Blogtalk
Reading statuses and notes
Allowing my words to heal
Constant support for the art and the artists
Think about crying
Like the leaves fall in autumn
Not because of unhappiness
But excited
Of what I have become

My own voice irritates me
No one around to join me
Speaking to myself
Of various decisions to make
Seems I am always at odds
With the younger, older and oldest
Sides of me
Will I really be loved by him?
Does it take them to love because of my commitment?

Therapeutic Stitches of a Heartbeat

My words serenades the inner vision
Accepting those around
Allowing the lessons
Spoke to be a testimony
Others to strive through the struggle
I often look at the younger me and smile
Understanding the older
Embracing the oldest

We know how to love thyself as well as him
Don't need many just that special one
But we are patient with love and life for the eruption of
this Poet and Person

FOR EVER

I thought I saw you today
Sun shined upon my head
Trees swayed as I walked by
Fallen leaves run upwards
The universe has accepted the love from you
Release me to be free
Not from the uncertainty
But to accept everything
Your whispers tiptoe upon my skin
Presence fill me from inside out
Safe and secure
Strong but sensitive with your touch
Provide me the simplest things for a smile
No one ever paid attention to my soul
Turn me on even with a tear
Comfort me until I am submerged
For I am in love with loving you
Hold me like shackles
That once confined my heart
Taking my hand
Leading me
Pulling me into your abyss of happiness
Our minds
Made love upon the clouds
Before our names had an and
The notes swept me away... (Beats)
My guard is secured with you
Daily means forever

I AM LISTENING

Mother Earth spoke softly today to me
One of her daughters with a destiny,
Whispering upon the back of a shifting breeze;
"Ahh, if you are the Queen Bee then your colony is all
that you need so don't be troubled with your intentions.
Keep the eye on the prize, and harvest the respect of
your people as no sequel will equal your own purpose.
Do not allow the observation of the ant, worm, wasp
nor fly distract your attention from the sacred
connection between self and the shape that holds your
worship. Hexagon holds order within one's dimension
do not become undone by the geometry spun by another
as all is balanced as long as you can find the pride to
stay alive and empowered. For in this moment Queen
Bee, your majesty is all that one can account for. With
tenacity it seems that some search for more, yet
alignment is the true assignment of the soul.
Adrina, can you remain focused?"

Mother Earth, "I have no desire for blasphemy nor
suggest that there could possibly be, an existence other
than my own that is more suited to me. I have no
impulse to become out of sync with the pleasure of true
contentment, just to replace my knowledge of
belonging with a longing of becoming something else.
No, mine is a divine purpose indeed, and as I am, I am
blessed to be!

And I am listening; to the pause, to the break, to the
space in between, to the thought that constructs the
dream. I'm listening; to the silence, to the sound, to the
gap between the words, to the intention of the verbs.
And I am witnessing; to the for, the against, the
balancing on the fence, the true observers of my events.

Ms Creoleness

I'm witnessing; to the energy, the source, the staying aligned, the veering off course. And I'm understanding. Hindsight extending my insight to the foresight of inner visions. I guess I'm overstanding.

As a poet, I hold stance and standard of ideas or ideals, when dealing with the vibrations of others. More to the point, I care about what I say. The power of words. The possibility of words. The responsibility of words. As a member of my family, and my community, I am aligned to the realty of being a Mother, a Daughter, a Sister, a Grandmother, and, a Friend. In short, I am all of the above, before, during and after I am an artist. I bow to the truth that poetry is my breath, and therefore find strength in the humility of the journey of independence and self-ownership. As my soul matures, I know there is more to be destined to me only for me.

Thank you Mother Earth for acknowledging me…

MISS HIM

I remember when your voice would give me chills
Through the snow, the spring and flowers blooming in
the winter
Your name would roll out of my mouth with ease
Concern not of someone taking my place in your heart

My thoughts became your words
Your actions became my will
Your face appeared among the clouds and petals
Then it hit me

It was a blow not only to my face but my soul
You loved me, I thought
I loved you, I know
Reality has come to surface
I was only there for a moment
Still…I stayed
Not out of love but contentment

Settling thinking,
"I don't want to date again, trust again"
"Speak my life again or even try to love again"
Miss him enough not to move past the good and bad
from him and with him
Sooner or later I will have issues carried to the next one

Years passed…..

Missed him now enough for his smile and body to be
replaced
He no longer creeps in my slumber to shadow you
The one who makes my eyes smiles in a fog
I am so fortunate that I was able to miss him enough to
find you.

DOOR

Who says that a smile couldn't end the war?
Of the heart and soul in the abyss calling for
True words with true actions nothing more
But a possibility of that feeling entered the door

A movable barrier opened the chains to a drawer
At a time to know every part from ceiling to floor
To appreciate the strength and my flaws adore
Me to be only me through his eyes I am spoken for

Be the shoulder for a few tears internally explore
When my arms touch others from your presence feeling
pour
To my lips to taste only the essence from the core
Because of him, I am no longer negative about love
anymore

Persuaded by the one who makes me sing a musical
score
Or maybe the best New Orleans Baker perfecting a
praline petit four
This man holds a key to the ultimate candy store
For he has unchained my heart, opened my soul and
behind him is the closed door.

CLOSURE

I sometime wonder
The words spoken upon sight
For the pain and tears
Played like a limp dog
Before the image
Of kicking you in the mouth
It took me years to forgive
But couldn't see past the hurt you gave to forgive
myself
I know how the game is played
But never thought you would change the rules
Of bench warming and technical fouls
My my, how the lies were told
Tried reverse psychology or attempted stupidity
Not realizing that I cried more than smile
Upon your presence
I defiled myself
Sometimes I wonder
The words spoken upon sight
Nah, I am good
Since I wasn't good for the truth then
No words are needed now.

Provided my own closure

ACKNOWLEDGMENTS

First and Foremost, THANK YOU to my Heavenly Father for bringing me through so much turmoil and strife to appreciate the gift of my strokes in Poetry.

My Father, Alex Smith, for SPITTING throughout my life, THANK YOU for passing on the veins for my ink (Still a Daddy's Girl).

To my Daughter Chane and Granddaughter Jordynn A HUGE MOM/NAWNI HUG AND THANK YOU for understanding the late nights of writing and Poetry Venue Hopping.

To my Mother, Betty Thomas, and Brother, Kareem Smith, for understanding what needed to be done for me to feel complete.

To GodChild the Omen and Seven Pierce for allowing a Brand New Poet the chance to be a voice of her own therapy (WET SPOT FILLED THANKS).

To my Friend and Supporter for always being a call or text away when I am about to jack something help.. No better love than from a MADDPOET

James "MrSpeaker Sears for being more than my Poetic Battle but a Friend.

James Myrick, Trina Davis-Butler and Yvonne Waller for always ready to support me, no matter if the words spoken made them blush.

To all of my 757 Poets and Poetry Venues from Richmond, Chesapeake, Newport News, Hampton, Portsmouth, Norfolk and Virginia Beach, THANK YOU for your love, support and artistic travels.

Therapeutic Stitches of a Heartbeat

To all of my Family, Friends, Soldiers, Veterans and Facebook Supporters, MAJOR THANK YOU for your undivided attention, listening ears, attentive eyes and endless nights.

THANK YOU to One Positive Way Radio, Def Poetry Speak; Inspirational Xpressionz, Penology Ink, No Chaser Radio, Verbal Collision, Scorpio Sessions, WKPJB Radio, Night Walks, Butterflies of the Pen for the opportunity to speak among the airwaves.

THANKS to all of my SHIPMATES and the Fellow Poets for riding the waves with me.

HUGS AND KISSES to my Son, Pierre and Daughter, Brandi for listening and laughing with me during this overdue project.

THANKS to LenzCapture Photography for the almost cover (Still shedding tears when I see this art.

A SPECIAL THANKS to Flenardo Taylor for being more than the Epitome of my Best Friend but my #1 Supporter. Who not only pushes me emotionally but mentally despite my past obstacles. You encourages me to bust through walls instead of waiting for an opened door, to cry when I am happy, smile when I am sad, stay calm when others don't share the level of my passion and above all to Love.

Once again, THANK YOU everyone for supporting this rebirth process of my struggles.

Until Then,
Never allow anyone to break you down until your spirit can't repair the pieces.

www.ingramcontent.com/pod-product-compliance
Lightning Source LLC
Chambersburg PA
CBHW071735020426
42331CB00008B/2039